When

God is
Silent

When God is Silent

Kellie Lane

CREATION HOUSE

WHEN GOD IS SILENT by Kellie Lane
Published by Creation House
A Charisma Media Company
600 Rinehart Road
Lake Mary, Florida 32746
www.charismamedia.com

Unless otherwise noted, all Scripture quotations are from the King James Version of the Bible.

Scripture quotations marked NIV are from the Holy Bible, New International Version. Copyright © 1973, 1978, 1984, 2010, 2011, International Bible Society. Used by permission.

Scripture quotations marked NKJV are from the New King James Version of the Bible. Copyright © 1979, 1980, 1982 by Thomas Nelson, Inc., publishers. Used by permission.

Scripture quotations marked NLT are from the Holy Bible, New Living Translation, copyright © 1996. Used by permission of Tyndale House Publishers, Inc., Wheaton, IL 60189. All rights reserved.

Design Director: Bill Johnson
Cover design by Terry Clifton

Visit the author's website: www.kellielane.org

Library of Congress CataloginginPublication Data: 2013946758
International Standard Book Number: 978-1-62136-677-5
E-book International Standard Book Number: 978-1-62136-678-2

First edition

13 14 15 16 17 — 987654321
Printed in the United States of America

Dedication

This book is dedicated to my mother
Chiquita Marie; a woman of strength,
courage, and tenacity. It was my mother
who reminded me of who I am in Christ
and that through Him I can do all things.

Table of Contents

Introduction

I know now, Lord, why you utter no answer. You yourself are the answer.

—C. S. Lewis[1]

If you're reading this book, more than likely you are in what is called a pressed place; a place of waiting. Does it seem as if God has forgotten about you? Has everyone else around you begun to celebrate their miracles, yet you are still crying yourself to sleep at night? Are you feeling a sense of weariness and emptiness? Have you been praying and crying out to God day in and out and still you see no change? Have you found yourself wondering if God has gone on vacation? Have you been contemplating that perhaps what you are believing God for is not in His will? Well if this describes you, congratulations! You are next in line for a miracle. I decree and declare defeat is not your portion; victory *is* your portion. Receive it, in Jesus' name. Amen.

What the enemy wants us to believe is that God will never answer our prayers. The kingdom of darkness works overtime as we get closer to our breakthroughs. Satan and his generals know that if he can get us to lose our focus, we will not be in position when the fullness of time comes and we will miss the blessing. We must know without a doubt that God is faithful and never fails. We must be certain that even if God is not talking, He's still listening. For it is written:

> But verily God hath heard me; he hath attended to the voice of my prayer.
>
> —Psalm 66:19

The psalmist knew that God had heard his prayer. This is because God will hear the prayer of the humble and the broken hearted who cry out to Him. It does not matter what you may have done in your past; if Jesus Christ is Lord of your life, God hears you. When we pray to our Father, we must go to Him in humility and in confession. We must trust and have faith that not only does He hear our secret petitions, but that He will grant them. We must give all that we have and all that we are to the Holy One; the only wise God. We must believe that the God who answers by fire will answer our petitions. For it is written:

> Blessed be God, which hath not turned away my prayer, nor his mercy from me.
>
> —Psalm 66:20

It is such a privilege to have twenty-four hour access to a God who will never take His loving kindness from us and who will never turn away our prayers. As followers of Christ, we sometimes have to remind ourselves of who God really is. Nothing is too hard for Him. Even what's impossible for man, is possible for God. We must also thank God for Jesus; it is because of Him that our prayers are answered.

Why I Wrote This book

I WROTE THIS BOOK from a pressed place. I wanted my personal experience of dealing with the agony of God being silent to bring forth deliverance for others. There were many times during this book writing that I wanted to give up. There were many days and nights that I declared God's promises to you in spite of my broken heart and a face filled with tears. But God! He's so faithful. Be encouraged and of good cheer. God has not forgotten about you. I can assure you that God will step in right on time. He is a faithful God who answers prayer.

CHAPTER 1

Why Is Heaven Shut Up?

There is a higher power, a higher influence,
a God who rules and reigns and controls
circumstances and situations that are beyond
your area and realm of authority.

—T. D. Jakes[1]

And the LORD, he it is that doth go before thee; he
will be with thee, he will not fail thee, neither forsake thee: fear not, neither be dismayed.

—DEUTERONOMY 31:8

YOU MAY BE at a point in your life where you feel aban-
doned by God. Not only have your prayers gone unanswered but it also seems as if heaven too has been shut up.
When faced with a situation like this, it may seem as if
time is standing still. Such times are extremely frustrating
and difficult to endure. During these times you may cry
out to God in prayer over and over yet nothing. God says
nothing. It appears as if God has become totally uninter-
ested in your tears, your pain, and your petitions. Has God
really turned a deaf ear to you? You may be asking, "God,
have you forgotten about me? Why won't You answer?"

Before we can expect to receive anything from God, we must first repent for our sins and clean house. God cannot dwell in an unclean temple. He has no choice but to turn His face from sin. Let's take a look at what Scripture says to support this:

> If I regard iniquity in my heart, the Lord will not hear me.
>
> —Psalm 66:18

> The Lord is far from the wicked: but he heareth the prayer of the righteous.
>
> —Proverbs 15:29

We know that all have sinned and fallen short of His glory, but thank God for the blood of Jesus. It is through the blood of Jesus, our faith in Him, and our repentant hearts that our sins are washed away. The Bible says:

> If we say that we have fellowship with him, and walk in darkness, we lie, and do not the truth. But if we walk in the light, as he is in the light, we have fellowship one with another, and the blood of Jesus Christ his Son cleanseth us from all sin. If we say that we have no sin, we deceive ourselves, and the truth is not in us. If we confess our sins, he is faithful and just to forgive us our sins, and to cleanse us from all unrighteousness.
>
> —1 John 1:6–9

After our sins have been confessed, we can then come boldly before the throne of grace and present our case blameless before the Father. It is then that we can have confidence that He hears and will answer according to His will and in His timing.

Let us pray:

> *Father God, in the name of Jesus, we come before You now acknowledging that You are the true and living God. We reverence You and only You. Today, Father, we confess our sins and ask for Your forgiveness. We ask to be washed in the blood of Jesus. Father, we thank You that we now have clean hearts and the right spirit to receive answers to our prayers. In Jesus' name we have prayed. Amen.*

After confession of sins, it's best to analyze our motives of why we are asking God for what we are asking for. Too often our prayers are motivated by selfishness such as, "Dear God, please give me that BMW I always wanted." Now, there's nothing wrong with believing God for a vehicle. There's nothing wrong with being specific about what you ask for. However, we must be mindful that our petitions are not totally self-centered. The Book of James tells us:

> Ye ask, and receive not, because ye ask amiss, that ye may consume it upon your lusts.
>
> —JAMES 4:3

Prayer that is totally self-centered does not fall under the promises of Jesus. We should request things that are of God and not merely to satisfy our selfish desires.

A better prayer would be:

> *Father God, I am believing you for a BMW. I understand according to Your Word that if I delight myself in You, the desires of my heart will be granted. If it not be in Your will for me to receive this particular car for whatever reason or that if my heart may somehow turn to stone once I receive it, then I ask that ultimately Your perfect will be done. I know that Your perfect will is what works best for me.*

When we look to find comfort in the Scripture we often turn to the Book of Job. Most Christians are familiar with this book of the Bible. You'll often hear believers who are going through difficult times describe their experience as "a Job experience." This Old Testament story reminds us of what happens when you cry out to God for answers and receive silence in exchange. You hardly hear about the fact that Job cried out to God for the first thirty seven chapters of the Book of Job and yet received no answer. When God finally spoke in the thirty-eighth chapter, He did so in a much unexpected manner. Let's take a look:

> Then the LORD answered Job out of the whirlwind, and said, Who is this that darkeneth counsel by words without knowledge? Gird up now thy loins like a man; for I will demand of thee, and answer thou me. Where wast thou when I laid the foundations of

the earth? declare, if thou hast understanding. Who hath laid the measures thereof, if thou knowest? or who hath stretched the line upon it? Whereupon are the foundations thereof fastened? or who laid the corner stone thereof; When the morning stars sang together, and all the sons of God shouted for joy? Or who shut up the sea with doors, when it break forth, as if it had issued out of the womb? When I made the cloud the garment thereof, and thick darkness a swaddling band for it, And break up for it my decreed place, and set bars and doors, And said, Hitherto shalt thou come, but no further: and here shall thy proud waves be stayed? Hast thou commanded the morning since thy days; and caused the dayspring to know his place; That it might take hold of the ends of the earth, that the wicked might be shaken out of it? It is turned as clay to the seal; and they stand as a garment. And from the wicked their light is withholden, and the high arm shall be broken. Hast thou entered into the springs of the sea? or hast thou walked in the search of the depth? Have the gates of death been opened unto thee? or hast thou seen the doors of the shadow of death? Hast thou perceived the breadth of the earth? declare if thou knowest it all.

—Job 38:1–18

At last, Job was granted his desire to have an audience with God. Yet, Job quickly realized it was not what he expected. God challenged Job to answer a series of questions posed in rapid succession regarding creation and nature. Job immediately realized God's great power and infinite wisdom. Job became overwhelmed and later admits his unworthiness to answer the Most High God. God asked Job, "Where were you when I laid the foundations of the Earth? Tell me, if you know so much" (1:4, NLT).

God may be telling you the same thing today. Often times we feel as if we know the way the story should end. We feel as if we have the solution and can't figure out why God is taking so long. The truth of the matter is we lack the cognitive ability to make sensible judgments concerning our future or even our present, for that matter. We must be mindful of the fact that our thoughts are not His thoughts neither are our ways His ways (Isa. 55:8). We have to remember that God knows our end from the beginning. We were not around when He laid the foundation of the Earth. "The earth is the LORD's, and the fullness thereof; the world, and they that dwell therein" (Ps. 24:1). Our lives are not our own. Therefore we must accept God's will regardless of how it feels. If God is silent, there is a reason. If no signs from heaven are available, know and understand that there is a very good reason for this also.

Let's take a look at the Book of Psalms:

> Hear my prayer, O LORD, and let my cry come unto thee. Hide not thy face from me in the day when I am in trouble; incline thine ear unto me: in the day when I call answer me speedily. For my days are consumed like smoke, and my bones are burned as an hearth. My heart is smitten, and withered like

grass; so that I forget to eat my bread. By reason of the voice of my groaning my bones cleave to my skin. I am like a pelican of the wilderness: I am like an owl of the desert. I watch, and am as a sparrow alone upon the house top.

—Psalm 102: 1–7

I'm sure you can relate to the psalmist in one way or another. The psalmist seems to be asking, "God, are you even listening to me or is Your face hidden? I'm pouring myself out to You and You don't appear to be moved. Can't You see my deep anguish? O, Lord, I'm hurting! Please, please, please notice me! Please hear my prayers! Please answer me, let me know that I have been noticed." The psalmist lets us know that it is quite alright to tell the Lord exactly how you feel. He's knows our feelings anyway. We don't have to hide or pretend that everything is okay when we feel as if we are dying on the inside. Remember, we serve a God who is all seeing and all knowing. We don't have to hide our expressions from Him.

Not hearing from God can be very trying. It can wear even the strongest, most mature saints down. During these times, we must turn to God's Word for comfort and instruction. We must stay rooted and grounded in His promises. We must recognize and respect His sovereignty and omnipotent power. God doesn't have to answer if He chooses not to. Yet because He loves us so much, He will not leave us in silence for longer than we can withstand.

There are many reasons why God may not have answered just yet. Just as people may choose to keep quiet for various reasons, God, too, may decide to keep quiet. If we, in our limited ability to reason, know when to speak and when not to, what can we expect from our wonderful Counselor? He will answer when the timing is right. We must not trouble ourselves with trying to figure out when He will speak. What is most important is that we are in a position to be able to hear and recognize the answer when it comes. We must get rid of all the clutter and distraction in our lives. We must shift our focus to Him and what He may be speaking through His most Holy Word. We must develop intimacy with Him. Perhaps that's what all the silence is about. It very well could be that God wants more alone time with us. Whatever the situation may be, God has promised to never leave us or forsake us. We must learn to be patient and very attentive. Then we will be able to hear the still small voice that may have been speaking all along.

CHAPTER 2

Faith and a Dime

Faith, mighty faith, the promise sees,
And looks to God alone; Laughs at
impossibilities, And cries it shall be done.

—CHARLES WESLEY[1]

F AITH IS A divine law. It supersedes the law of works and the law of sin and death. The same faith that was required to confess Jesus as Lord with your mouth and to believe in your heart that God raised Him from the dead is the same faith needed to bring victory into your life today. If you have not confessed Jesus as Lord of your life, let's take a moment and do that now. Please pray this prayer with me:

> *Father God, I come to You in the name of Jesus. I*
> *acknowledge to You that I am a sinner, and I ask Your*
> *forgiveness; I need Your forgiveness.*
>
> *I believe that Your only begotten Son, Jesus Christ,*
> *shed His blood on the cross at Calvary and died for*
> *my sins.*

You said in Your Holy Word, Romans 10:9, that if
we confess the Lord our God and believe in our hearts
that God raised Jesus from the dead, we shall be saved.
    Right now I confess Jesus as the Lord of my life.
With my heart I believe that You raised Jesus from the
dead. This very moment I accept Jesus Christ as my
own personal Savior; and according to His Word, right
now I declare that I am saved.
    Thank you, Lord Jesus, for Your unlimited grace
which has saved me from my sins. Now, Father God, I
ask You to transform my life so that I may bring glory
and honor to You alone. Amen.

Scripture teaches us that without faith it is impossible to please God (Heb. 11:6). Without faith there can be no attainment of strength, no permanent security. Most of us know and understand this, yet we still struggle. One day we stand in faith and believe God, the next day we become anxious and fearful that God will not answer. Doubt enters our mind. We must understand that faith has absolutely nothing to do with our physical senses. You have to believe God when the odds are stacked against you. Our prayers are first answered in the realm of the spirit. It requires faith to pull it down. You have to believe God when your natural reasoning says it'll never come to pass. When those thoughts enter your mind, you must replace them with "but God." It may seem as if I will never receive my miracle—but God. The God we serve is the God who answers by fire. You can rest assured that He will bring it to pass. Our God is a great God who gives good gifts to His children. If you ask for bread, will He give you a stone? No He will not. We just have to trust Him.

My spiritual mother once believed God for a new car. She dreamed of being at a nearby car lot picking out what she wanted. The next morning she awakened with confidence that God had spoken to her. Off to the car lot she went. She picked out what she wanted and then completed the application process. She had no money for a down payment but still waited with excitement. She could not wait to drive off in her brand new vehicle. The car salesman eventually informed her of the status of her application. He apologetically informed her that her application had been denied.

She politely thanked the gentleman for his time. She left the car lot thanking God. She thanked Him for His goodness, and she also thanked Him for her new car. She said she was more excited when she left the car lot than she was when she got there. She knew that if God showed it to her, He would bring it to pass. She had the faith to celebrate denial. She knew that a *no* at that car lot meant nothing to a God of whom everything is possible. She thanked God for three days for her new vehicle. On the evening of the third day, she played the dream back in her head and realized she did not go to the specific car lot that God had revealed to her in her dream.

We have to understand that God is a God of specificity. We have to learn how to pay close attention to every detail that He shows us. The next day she went to that specific car lot. She only had ten cents in her pocket. When she walked in, a gentleman greeted her. He asked her how he could help her. She told him she was there to purchase a vehicle.

He asked, "How much money do you have?"

She replied, "All I have is faith and a dime."

He smiled and told her, "If that's what God sent you with, then that must be all that you need." She again completed the application process and the waiting began. The salesman told her he would get back with her with the status as soon as he heard back from financing.

She went home again claiming the victory in Christ Jesus. That night, God gave her another dream. This time the Lord showed her a key ring with three keys on it. In the dream she jumped up and caught the keys as they descended from heaven.

Sometimes what we believe God for requires a leap of faith. You have to trust God enough to reach for the answer to your prayer. The following morning around 9 a.m. she received a phone call from the salesman letting her know that her vehicle was ready for pick up. When she arrived at the car lot, she was handed a key ring with three keys on it, just as God had shown her in the dream.

How faithful is our God! She could have given up when the first car lot denied her. But instead, she praised God even the more. We have to have the kind of faith that speaks to the mountains in our lives and commands them to be thou removed and they be cast into the sea (Matt. 17:20). When it seems as if the door has been slammed in your face, have faith and know that there must be another entrance. Seek God for the passage way. This is why scripture teaches us to walk by faith and not by sight (2 Cor. 5:7).

Let us pray:

> *Father God, in the name of Jesus, bless us with the gift of faith. We understand that without it we cannot please You. We know that with it, all things are possible. Give us the ability to reach for the answers to our prayers. In Jesus name we have prayed. Amen.*

CHAPTER 3

Warning: Watch Your Mouth

*You can change your world by changing
your words... Remember, death and life
are in the power of the tongue.*
—JOEL OSTEEN[1]

EVER BEEN AROUND someone who speaks negative all of the time? I pray that person is not sitting in your clothes. Words have power. This is why we must be careful to filter our vocabulary. All evil comes forth from the heart and proceeds out of the mouth. For it is written:

> The heart is deceitful above all things, and desperately wicked: who can know it?
> —JEREMIAH 17:9

> For out of the abundance of the heart the mouth speaketh.
> —MATTHEW 12:34

So how do we gain control over our tongues? We must first experience spiritual circumcision of the heart. Then the evil that comes out of our hearts will cease (Rom: 2:29). For it is written:

And I will give them one new heart, and I will put
a new spirit within you; and I will take the stony
heart out of their flesh, and will give them an heart
of flesh.

—Ezekiel 11:19

Let's take a moment to pray:

*Father God, we know You as a master Surgeon.
Humbly we ask You, O God, to perform open heart
surgery on us. Remove every hidden impurity and
wash us clean in the mighty name of Jesus. Amen.*

I once counseled with a lady who was believing God to
restore her marriage. Let's call her Mary. In addition to
Mary fighting for her marriage, she was also fighting for
her life. Mary had stage IV breast cancer at the time and
had no positive results with chemotherapy.

Do you not know that the enemy does not fight fair?
He "kicks you" when you're already down. That's why we
have to fight back with the Word of God. Mary said she
couldn't believe what was once so good had turned so bad.
She honestly couldn't figure out where things went wrong.
Her husband had become involved with another woman
and had a child with her. Mary was distraught but was
convinced that she still wanted her marriage. The husband
was actively involved with the mistress but still lived at
home with his wife. She said when things got really bad,
he simply moved to the other side of the house. She said

her home has a very awkward floor plan and it was almost as if they lived in two separate quarters.

She sat in my office, leaned her head back, and began to weep. I remember getting up from my desk, going to her, kneeling down in front of her, and reminding her that God had not forgotten about her. I told her if she wanted her marriage, then to declare it; speak life into what appeared to be a dead situation. It didn't matter what it looked like. I began to tell her about how much power her words carry. I told her we can bless or curse our life by every word that proceeds out of our mouth. I told her that every time she spoke a word that is not fruitful, she made a covenant with the devil. I told her he then has to honor his end of the deal. All of a sudden she looked at me so strange.

I asked her, "What is it?"

She said, "You're exactly right! From the time we purchased the home, I have always said how much I loved my house and its awkward floor plan. I would always tell people when my husband decides he doesn't want me anymore, he can simply pack up and move to the other side of the house."

I immediately began to pray with her. We had to break the covenant she made with the enemy out of ignorance. This is why the Bible teaches us that we are destroyed because of a lack of knowledge (Hosea 4:6). Here's another example:

My mother birthed three children. My sister is three and one-half years older than I am. My brother is thirteen years younger. My mother was thirty-six years old at the time of my brother's arrival. For many years my mother worried that she would not live long enough to see her son grow up because he was so much younger than her other two children. She began to pray that God would allow her to live just long enough to see him become an adult. She later told me that she always feared that she would die an untimely death. She was so fearful that she felt like she would just make a deal with God. If she could see my brother graduate high school, she would be satisfied. That fear is what stimulated her prayer. What my mother didn't realize is that fear is not of God. For it is written:

> For God hath not given us the spirit of fear; but of power, and of love, and of a sound mind.
> —2 Timothy 1:7

About a month after my baby brother graduated high school, my mother began to experience urinary frequency. She didn't think much of it at first since she's a nurse. I remember her coming to visit one day and literally having to use the restroom about ten times in thirty minutes. Well, over the course of about a week things took a turn for the absolute worst. She was evaluated by a urologist and diagnosed with stage III bladder cancer.

Yes, just like that. Do you realize that the course of your life can change in an instant? I cannot begin to describe the feeling that pierced my heart. How could this be? Not my mother. I was totally devastated. I mean, I just knew for sure that my mother would live forever. At least that's what I secretly believed. How could this happen? She was always so healthy. I had no idea of the prayer my mother had been praying for the last eighteen years.

About nine months later, after failed chemotherapy and radiation, I was in a hotel room with my mother reading the Word of God. I was led to the scripture about life or death being in our tongue. I began to witness to my mother about how much power our words carry. I began to explain to her that if she truly wanted her life, she could have it. I told her that all she had to do was speak a word in faith and it would be done. It was then that she confessed her prayer.

I thank God for revelation. I thank God that He led me to that specific scripture on that particular night. It was an on time word for my mother's situation. That night my mother opened her mouth and told God that she changed her mind. We broke covenant with the devil. We cancelled every word spoken out of her mouth against her life in ignorance. We covered her body in the blood of Jesus and declared her healing. Glory be to God, my mother is alive and well today.

If you've ever spoken anything out of your mouth in ignorance against your life, today is your day to break covenant. Right now, wherever you are, take a moment, lift your hands, open your mouth, and declare:

> *I break covenant with the devil. I cancel every lifeless word that has ever proceeded out of my mouth due to ignorance. Father God, forgive me for every idle word*

*(Matt. 12:36); saturate me in Your blood. In Jesus
name I have prayed. Amen.*

You know the childhood saying, "Sticks and stones may
break my bones, but words will never harm me." Well now
we know that is an untruth. Words can harm us. Since
this is true, then the reverse of this fact is also true. If
the tongue has the ability to defile and tear down, then
with the same tongue we can also bless and edify. For this
reason, we must begin to speak fruitful things.

After our heart undergoes spiritual circumcision, we
can then speak out and declare the truth of what God's
Word reveals to us. We must learn to shift our focus from
the problem to the Problem Solver. Our Father God, the
only God who answers by fire, will answer. If we continue to speak things based on natural circumstances, we
will never get relief. If we continue to focus on how bad
things really are, we're declaring what's happening in the
natural and not what God promises to give us according
to His Word.

Speaking His Word concerning a situation will bring
about the desired change. We must understand that the
"word of God is quick, and powerful, and sharper than
any twoedged sword" (Heb. 4:12). We must learn to speak
the Word over our situation until we see His promises fulfilled. Each time we speak God's Word, angels are acti-
vated on our behalf. Be patient. As long as you're in His
will, He's going to bring justice to you. For it is written:

And whatsoever ye shall ask in my name, that will
I do, that the Father may be glorified in the Son.

—JOHN 14:13

And shall not God avenge his own elect, which cry
day and night unto him, though he bear long with
them.

—LUKE 18:7

CHAPTER 4

Don't Put God in the Trunk

If anyone is ashamed of me and my words, the Son of Man will be ashamed of him when he comes in his glory and in the glory of the Father and of the holy angels.

—LUKE 9:26

E VER HEARD OF the story about the girls who put God in the trunk? Well, just in case you haven't, let me share it with you. One evening a few girls decided they would go out for a night of joy riding and dating. As the girls got into the car, the mother of one of the girls walked her outside. She told her, "Remember to let God ride with you." The daughter replied in a joking manner, "If God is going to ride with us, He'd better get in the trunk because there's no room in here." The girls laughed and drove away. Later that night, the young ladies were involved in a fatal car crash. No one survived. The car was beyond recognition, with the exception of the trunk. The trunk was completely intact without a scratch. When the police saw the trunk, they were astounded. They opened it. Inside they found a crate of eggs. Not one egg was cracked.[1]

Have you ever left God in the trunk? I know that the story above seems to be extreme. But many of us do the exact same thing every single day. We deny Christ anytime we profess to be Christians but fail to live up to it. The apostle Paul wrote:

> They profess that they know God; but in works they deny him, being abominable, and disobedient, and unto every good work reprobate.
>
> —Titus 1:16

I once worked with a lady who was so angry all of the time. She did a good job with her work assignment but would fire off at the mouth over any little thing. Once in an in-service meeting, she came unglued because she was not recognized for her work ethics. She was so furious because she was not selected that she walked up to another employee in front of everyone in the meeting and shouted, "How did he get the award but I didn't?" She stormed out of the meeting.

We must realize that what is our portion is our portion. When God is for us there's not a force in hell that can be against us. With that being said, we should rejoice and celebrate the blessings of our brothers and sisters. We should be able to rest in the assurance that in due season we too shall reap our reward if we stay faithful. We are never to covet what does not belong to us. Why would God ever choose to bless us if we feel as if even what belongs to someone else should be ours? This is why we must have a personal, intimate relationship with our Savior. We must know with our "knower" that God is in the blessing business and will never withhold any good thing from those whose walk is blameless (Ps. 84:11).

Now back to the story of the angry coworker. A few weeks later others received a promotion but she didn't. Her abrupt, inappropriate behavior during the meeting was not the reason for her not receiving the promotion. It just so happened that she was not promoted; some reasons were more obvious than others. She phoned my desk to ask why she was not chosen. I began to tell her that if she would do her work as unto the Lord, in due season she would reap her harvest. I explained that God promotes.

She cut me off mid sentence and said, "Now wait one minute, I believe in God; but when I come to work I leave Him outside of the doors. I don't work for God; I work for man." She then went on to say, "You had better be careful talking about God all the time."

I was shocked! After I picked my mouth up from the floor, I told her, "Ma'am, you called my desk. Anyone who calls my desk and asks me for advice or insight will hear about my God. And I wouldn't advise you to continue leaving God outside of the doors. The time will come when He will no longer be waiting for you when you get off work."

Jesus tells us about a scenario similar to this in the thirteenth chapter of Luke. For it is written:

> Strive to enter in at the narrow gate: for many, I say unto you, will seek to enter in, and shall not be able. When once the Master of the house is risen up, and

hath shut the door, and ye begin to stand without, and to knock at the door, saying, Lord, Lord, open unto us; and he shall answer and say unto you, I know not whence ye are: Then shall ye begin to say, We have eaten and drunk in thy presence, and thou hast taught in our streets. But he shall say, I tell you, I know not whence ye are; depart from me, all ye workers of iniquity.

—Luke 13: 24–26

We must realize that anyone who turns from the truth of God or rejects the Holy Spirit as a source of power has denied Christ. If we deny Christ before men, He will then deny us before the Father. For it is written:

But whoever shall deny me before men, him will I also deny before my Father which is in heaven.

—Matthew 10:33

Let us pray:

Father God, if there is any action, thought, or deed that is causing us to deny the power of Your Spirit, we ask first that You forgive us. We then ask for You to take away every unclean thing from our minds and hearts. We acknowledge You as the truth. There is none like You. Give us a heart that will rejoice when our brothers and sisters rejoice. Give us a heart that will allow us to dance when others are dancing. It is because of Your goodness, Your grace, Your mercy, and Your compassion that we are here today. Thank You for never turning Your back on us, even when

*we turned our back on You. We find comfort today
in knowing that You being for us is greater than
the whole world against us. In Jesus' name we pray.
Amen.*

CHAPTER 5

Pace Yourself

*The will to win means nothing if you
haven't the will to prepare.*
—JUMA IKANGAA[1]

H AVE YOU EVER wondered how a marathon runner trains? An expert will first tell you that until you have been consistently running for a least one year it is not recommended. During that year of preparation you should be training a minimum of four to five days a week averaging twenty-five miles per week. Even for the seasoned athlete, running a marathon race is an exhausting event. For beginners, the race can be grueling from start to finish. In addition to appropriate physical conditioning you have to have the right equipment for your planned race. You must have a good comfortable pair of running shoes that provide plenty of support. The soles of your shoes must also be good in order to absorb shock to your feet. Only a fool would attempt to run a marathon in a pair of brand new shoes. You would never make it to the finish line! Even your socks have to be thick and comfortable. You have to take weather into consideration as well. As a marathon runner, you have to be prepared for a whole realm of weather conditions that may occur. It could be extremely hot, rainy, windy, or extremely cold. Your clothing must be appropriate and as comfortable as possible. You have to drink plenty of water and increase caloric intake as you prepare. Your level of physical fitness will determine your endurance level. Your running times will need to increase as the time becomes near. Even under the perfect conditions, you should prepare at least four months in advance in order to be successful.[2]

Now you may be asking what a marathon runner has to do with my prayers being answered. What does running a race have to do with my walk with God? The preparation is actually very similar. The biggest mistake a believer can make is to run a spiritual race without adequate preparation and conditioning. Perhaps in your mind you are thinking, "If I petition God for a few days or a few weeks, He will answer me. If He doesn't then it must not be in His will." Well that is incorrect. God has promised us that He will answer our prayers. For it is written:

> Ask, and it shall be given you; seek, and ye shall find; knock, and it shall be opened unto you.
> —Matthew 7:7

Often times we are not physically or spiritually prepared to wait on the answer. If God answers in a few days, a few weeks, or sometimes in a few months, most of us can tough it out. But what happens when God doesn't answer in what we consider a timely manner? What happens when we grow weary? The Bible teaches us to not grow weary in our well doing for in due season we will reap if we faint not (Gal. 6:9). The most important thing that you can do if and when you find yourself in this type of situation is to remain in position.

As you're waiting for God to move, be mindful that positioning is very important. You can't be here, there, and everywhere and expect God to move. What do I mean by that? Let me give you an example of a story my friend once shared with me.

> There was once a man who died and went to heaven. As he walked the streets of gold he came upon a very tall door with his name written on it. He wondered what could possibly be inside. He pondered and pondered until eventually he asked an angel if he could he go inside. The angel responded, "You probably don't want to go in there." Well, the man insisted and was eventually granted his request. When he walked inside of the huge room, there were boxes piled as high as he could see and they were all labeled "return to sender." The man was very confused by this point and asked the angel what could be in all of these boxes? The angel replied, "Each box is filled with answers to your prayers. Every time you asked God for something; He gave it to you. But when the boxes were delivered to your address on Faith Street, no one was home. So the boxes were all returned."

Let us not be like the man in this story. Our prayer must be that we remain in the proper position to receive the answers to our prayers.

The Bible teaches us that if we ask God in faith and do not doubt, He will grant us whatever we ask (James 1:6). This is why we must run the race with endurance. We have to pace ourselves so that we don't give up and move out of position if God doesn't answer us right away. God honors persistence. For it is written:

> Wherefore seeing we also are compassed about with so great a cloud of witnesses, let us lay aside every weight, and the sin which doth so easily beset us, and let us run with patience the race that is set before us. Looking unto Jesus the author and finisher of our faith; who for the joy that was set before him endured the cross, despising the shame, and is set down at the right hand of the throne of God. For consider him that endured such contradiction of sinners against himself, lest ye be wearied and faint in your minds.
>
> —Hebrews 12:1–3

If God answered all of our prayers immediately, would we appreciate what He has given us? More than likely we would not. I remember how much money I used to spend on my children for Christmas. By New Year's Day half of the items were destroyed or thrown all over the floors in their rooms. If they visited someone's house during the holidays, they left items there. I remember buying my daughter an iPod three years straight. The same exact one. Each year she took it to her grandparents' home, and I never saw it again. Each year I would tell her if you lose it this time, that's it. Well, she would promise and promise to take better care the next time. But guess what? She lost it again and again. She didn't appreciate the gift. She was so used to me buying her whatever she wanted. She knew that if she lost it, I would replace it. Well, it's been several years since my daughter last had an iPod. She can really feel the pain now that all of her friends have one. The next time she gets an iPod, she will be able to purchase it herself. Do you think the iPod will then have more value? I'm sure it will. Well, if that's my method for teaching my daughters how to appreciate a gift, what more will our Father do for us?

Here's another example. I remember how badly I wanted a black on black GL 450 Mercedes truck. It was my "dream truck." The day I found the exact one that I wanted and purchased it, I was so very happy. I remember how carefully I used to park it in my garage. I told my children they had better not ride their bicycles close to it. I told them not to eat in it. I told them to keep their little finger prints off of the windows. Well, that lasted all of about two months. I look at my truck now and say, "It's a shame that I haven't washed you in months." I no longer value it the way that I did at first. I'm thankful for it, but that initial excitement is gone.

Some things that we believe God for require a lifelong commitment. For instance, if you're believing God for a child, once God blesses you with the child, you're a parent for life. You can't park the child in the garage and allow him or her to collect dust. If you're believing God for a restored marriage, once He does this, then what? Can you change your mind and pretend to be single again? No. If you're believing God for a spouse, once He grants the petition, what's next? What happens when disagreements occur? Do you give up? No, you don't! We must count the cost. God knows our end from the beginning. He's preparing us for the unseen. He uses our present circumstances for training, not punishment. For it is written:

> And ye have forgotten the exhortation which speaketh unto you as unto children, My son, despise not thou the chastening of the Lord, nor faint when thou art rebuked of him: For whom the Lord loveth he chasteneth, and scourgeth every son whom he receiveth. If ye endure chastening, God dealeth with you as with sons; for what son is he whom the father chasteneth not? But if ye be without chastisement, whereof all are partakers, then are ye bastards, and not sons. Furthermore we have had fathers of our flesh which corrected us, and we gave them reverence: shall we not much rather be in subjection unto the Father of spirits, and live? For they verily for a few days chastened us after their own pleasure; but he for our profit, that we might be partakers of his holiness. Now no chastening for the present seemeth to be joyous, but grievous: nevertheless afterward it yieldeth the peaceable fruit of righteousness unto them which are exercised thereby. Wherefore

lift up the hands which hang down, and the feeble knees; and make straight paths for your feet, lest that which is lame be turned out of the way; but let it rather be healed.

—HEBREWS 12:5–13

I remember when God placed it in my spirit to birth a prayer line. He gave me specific instructions on how the prayer line was to be handled. Birthing a prayer line seemed like a good idea to me. I was spending most of my time in prayer anyway and was not sleeping much. So I rounded up a couple of my closest prayer partners who agreed to join me and the intercession began. We began to see immediate results. Testimonies were coming forth every night. The number of people on the prayer line increased. We were going full speed until fatigue hit us. We would sometimes call the line and you could hear people snoring. I didn't mind the snoring, the spirit never sleeps. The point I'm trying to make is that we must pace ourselves. The flesh will rise up every time you attempt to make a commitment to God. The enemy will bring all sorts of distractions your way. You must stay focused. If you tell God that you're going to do something, you had better do it. The benefits will be beyond your wildest imagination if you just steady the course. If you become tired while trying to endure, ask the Lord for strength. He will grant your request.

Let us pray:

Father God, we humbly ask You for the ability to run our spiritual race with endurance. We ask You, Lord, for the grace to faint not. We understand that in our weakness You make us strong. Settle our spirits, dear Lord, so that we may be anxious for nothing. Anoint us to be in the proper position to receive the answers to our prayers. In Jesus' name. Amen.

CHAPTER 6

Help!

We shall steer safely through every storm, so long as our heart is right, our intention fervent, our courage steadfast, and our trust fixed on God.
—St. Francis De Sales[1]

H AVE YOU EVER come to a place in your life where you feel as if you've done all you can? You've prayed, fasted, believed, declared His Glory, sowed seeds, and waited and waited and waited; and still no physical manifestation? I can assure you from my own personal experience that being in this situation becomes very uncomfortable. Perhaps if God would give us a hint of how long this process was going to last, we might be able to somehow bear the pain.

I remember when my mom was going through aggressive chemotherapy she would always say, "I wonder how much more of this will I have to endure? I just pray that the tumors are gone when I go back the next time." She would tell me, "Kellie, I just don't know how much more I can handle, it's just too much!" When we first discussed a treatment plan with her oncologist, one of our first questions was: "How long do you anticipate that this whole process will last." Her oncologist then replied, "It could take weeks; it could takes months. It depends on how well your body responds."

When you're faced with a situation like this, you somehow have a ray of hope that you will fall into the category of the quickest recovery. But what do you do when the deliverance does not come quickly? What happens when days turn to weeks, weeks turn to months, and months sometimes turn to years? Did God change His mind? No! Has God become unfaithful? Absolutely not! We know that God never breaks a promise. If He said He's going to heal you, He's going to heal you. If He said He's going to deliver you, He's going to deliver you. If He said He's going to send you a godly spouse, He's going to do it. If He promised to restore your marriage, consider it done. But the question we all want answered is: "How long Lord?" We ponder, "How long do I have to watch everyone else celebrate and still no breakthrough for me? God, how long? I'm running out of strength. God, I'm running out of hope. I want to pray, but it seems like I'm losing the ability to even do that." You may feel as if you're all alone. When you find yourself in this situation, an emergency is declared in heaven.

Ever been in a public place and all of a sudden you hear the word *help*! What does everyone do? No matter who you are, you begin looking around and searching for whoever shouted those words. Obviously they need to be rescued. Ever witnessed a near drowning experience? When the person begins to drown, the victim desperately shouts "Help!!" There's no time to be cute, the person is fighting for his life. At that moment in time, it doesn't matter who's around. They don't care how silly they may look; all they know is if someone doesn't save them immediately, the next breath may be their last. Instantly the life guard flies off of his post and throws out a lifeline. Everyone else has to clear the water. The focus is shifted to the one who needs to be saved.

Do you feel in your spirit that the time has come for you to really get God's attention? You've believed God for everyone else, but now the focus must shift to you. You can become so desperate for God that it feels as if your life depends on it. If this describes your situation, you need a lifeline from heaven. You may feel like God has forgotten about you. You've run out of fancy prayers; you're tired. Nothing has moved for you. You're in a place of desperation. Who is the Guarder of life? Jehovah God, that's who! All you have to do is lift your head to heaven, and with a voice of triumph shout "Help!!!"

Now this is not an instruction for people who are still trying to be cute while waiting on the Lord. This is for the real believers who know that if God doesn't rescue you, the ship you're on is about to sink. You have gotten to a place where you could care less about what other people think. Right where you are, if this describes your circumstance, shout "Help" at the top of your lungs! Do it repeatedly until you feel a release. Know that our Father in heaven promises to help us. If a stranger who hears your distress will hurry to help you, what more will your Creator do for you? For it is written:

> May the LORD answer you when you are in distress;
> may the name of the God of Jacob protect you.
> —PSALM 20:1, NIV

Jehovah God is our Helper. But how can you get help if you don't ask for it? Don't give up now. If you're reading these words, know that you are next in line for a miracle. Please know and understand where your help comes from. There's a reason why no one else can help you. Sometimes God likes to show up and just be God all by Himself. God will sometimes allow situations to happen just so that He can show you that He is God. He enjoys making your life a wonder to everyone else around you. God will allow you to be backed into a corner with everyone watching just so He can get the glory out of your story. God sometimes likes an audience. Just know that right now He is setting the stage, and soon the curtain will rise. All will see that is was the hand of God upon your life. He is so worthy to be praised! Know that regardless of how you are feeling right now, your help is on the way.

Let us pray:

> *Father God, we thank You for Your loving kindness. We honor You for being a strategic planner. We recognize You as the CEO of the universe. Everything belongs to You. We understand that our lives are in*

Your hands. We know that You have not forgotten about us. We lift our hands to heaven right now and receive our help. Thank You for being our Helper, our Keeper, and the Lifter of our heads. In Jesus' name. Amen.

CHAPTER 7

A Delayed Blessing

Isn't it funny how something that will later be a
blessing can be a curse if you get it too soon?

—T. D. JAKES

To every thing there is a season, and a time to every
purpose under the heaven: A time to be born, and a
time to die; a time to plant, and a time to pluck up
that which is planted.

—ECCLESIASTES 3:1–2

HAVE YOU EVER been in a situation, or perhaps you
are in one right now, where you feel as if you can't
go another day if God doesn't answer you? As best you
know, you've done everything right; yet still nothing.
From personal experience I know this feeling all too well.
It can be very discouraging. You feel in your heart as if
there must be something else that you haven't done and
that's why God hasn't answered. You may be hearing
from those around you, "Just wait on Him." I'm sure at
some point you may even get a bit agitated because that's
exactly what you've been doing—waiting, and waiting, and
waiting. Well what do you do? You've been praying and

thanking God, you've been standing on His Word, you've done everything within your power to line up your life according to His will; yet it seems like God hasn't noticed any of your efforts.

I remember when one of my best friends was having trouble on her job. Her new supervisor was nothing short of evil. On the day the new supervisor was hired, my friend panicked. She recognized the lady from a previous place of employment. My friend told me that then she only worked with her five days before quitting because she was just awful. She would curse and shout at her employees and have them in tears. So, my friend already knew what she was up against. I remember telling her, "Let's take this to the Lord in prayer."

Let me tell you; my friend is not just a regular lady. She truly walks in the authority of Christ Jesus. She is favored everywhere that she goes. Everything that she puts her hands to prospers. So I knew that if this new supervisor started making trouble with her, the God who answers by fire was sure to intervene. Not only that, but the supervisor had no idea that my friend engaged nightly in midnight intercession on our prayer line. So not only was she barking up the wrong tree, she had no idea that my friend was surrounded by prayer warriors who reinforced her petitions to God. We began to pray at midnight that any force working against my friend on her job would be removed in Jesus' name. At the same time, just as expected, the supervisor began to nitpick. It was so bad that my friend would get an upset stomach at the thought of going to work. We continued to pray. In two weeks' time the new supervisor was fired.

Is God not an on time God? Does He not hurry to rescue His elect? If you are truly in an emergent situation, don't think for one moment that God will not make haste to rescue you. So, if He has not answered your petition just yet, it simply indicates that the fullness of time has not come. This is why we must wait on His promises to be fulfilled.

The dreaded waiting period often leaves a believer imbalanced emotionally. It's not that we don't believe that God is going to do what He said, we just don't know how long we have to endure. It reminds me of the "two week wait" couples experience when trying to conceive. After the small window of conception closes, the waiting begins. If they are blessed with a seed, a very complicated process begins to take place behind the scenes. At the moment of fertilization, the genes and sex of the baby are already set. Yet, it can take up to twenty weeks post conception for the sex of the baby to be determined via ultrasound. So, for the first twenty weeks does that mean that the developing fetus is not already a boy or a girl? No! It means that it's not time for the world to know just yet.

The same goes for you. When the fullness of time comes, Jehovah God will remove you from obscurity and all will know what you have been carrying. Then it will make perfect sense to you why the opposition has been so great. Just as God knows what He placed on the inside of you, the forces of darkness know it too. Don't rush the development of your "baby." Go through your process so that you can "deliver at full term."

From the time of conception, it takes another two weeks or so before a positive pregnancy test result will occur. What happens if the mother takes the pregnancy test too soon? That's right, the result will be negative. Is the woman pregnant? Yes, she is. Get my point? Even though the blessing has been released, it's too soon to yield a positive result. We must recognize that often times the miracles of God take time to manifest in the physical. It doesn't mean that He hasn't answered. Remember what happened in the Book of Daniel? Let's take a look at it:

> Then said he unto me, Fear not, Daniel: for from the first day that thou didst set thine heart to understand and to chasten thyself before thy God, thy words were heard, and I am come for thy words. But the prince of the kingdom of Persia withstood me one and twenty days: but, lo, Michael, one of the chief princes, came to help me; and I remained there with the kings of Persia.
>
> —DANIEL 10:12–13

There are demonic forces that can temporarily delay blessings or answers to prayer that must be destroyed for you to see blessings manifest. You can see from the scripture that this kingdom of the prince of Persia represents such. But beyond that, there is reinforcement from God capable of destroying them. There is no demonic force strong enough to snatch away God's promise to you. If you are currently experiencing severe opposition in any area of your life, know that promotion is next. The walls of Jericho fell; not by power nor might. It fell by the spoken Word of God. Let's take a look at the Book of Joshua:

> Now Jericho was straightly shut up because of the children of Israel: none went out, and none came in. And the Lord said unto Joshua, See, I have given into thine hand Jericho, and the king thereof, and the mighty men of valour. And ye shall compass the city, all ye men of war, and go round about the city once. Thus shalt thou do six days. And seven priests shall bear before the ark seven trumpets of rams' horns: and the seventh day ye shall compass the city seven times, and the priests shall blow with the trumpets. And it shall come to pass, that when they make a long blast with the ram's horn, and when ye hear the sound of the trumpet, all the people shall shout with a great shout; and the wall of the city shall fall down flat, and the people shall ascend up every man straight before him.
>
> —Joshua 6:1–5

That stronghold in your case is as good as fallen just as the wall of Jericho came tumbling down. No matter how long your prayer has gone unanswered or how stubborn your situation may seem, it's over. The Word of our God is settled in heaven. The Scripture cannot be broken. God is faithful and cannot lie. He is a promise keeper. He is the lifter of your head. The weapons of our warfare are mighty through God to the pulling down of strongholds

(1 Cor. 10:4). The precious blood of Jesus is a weapon that no stronghold can resist. What the enemy sends your way as stumbling blocks become your stepping stones. When the enemy comes one way, he will have to flee seven ways (Deut. 28:7). Daniel is a perfect example of the importance of persistence. Don't give up, you have been heard. Eventually God will send angelic forces to assist until you reach your point of breakthrough. Daniel's blessing was held up for twenty-one days. It was delayed but not denied. I'm telling you today; if you are upright and living a consecrated life, God heard your request the first time. He *will* answer you.

Let us pray:

> *Father God, we ask that You stir up holy rebellion in us that will allow us to travail to the point of breakthrough. If you be willing, Lord, give us a glimpse of what we are carrying. Help us to understand why the forces of darkness are working overtime to destroy us. We choose now to break the back of the strongman and demonic forces assigned to assassinate our destinies. We denounce every form of spiritual wickedness that could force us into preterm labor. We will carry our seeds full term so that You will get the glory, honor, and praise that are due unto You. We understand that Your timing is perfect. In Jesus' name we have prayed. Amen.*

CHAPTER 8

Praise Him in the Fire

Our entire being is fashioned as an instrument of praise. Just as a master violin maker designs an instrument to produce maximum aesthetic results, so God tailor-made our bodies, souls and spirits to work together in consonance to produce pleasing expressions of praise and worship. When we use body language to express praise, that which is internal becomes visible.

—Don McMinn[1]

IT TAKES VERY little effort to praise Jehovah God when everything is going well. However, can you praise Him in the fire? The Bible teaches us that in everything we are to give thanks for this is the will of God (1Thess. 5:18). The Word of God also teaches us that all things work together for the good of those who love God and are called according to His purpose (Rom. 8:28). This scripture in Romans is not simply speaking of the things that make us feel good. "All things" include the good, the bad, and the ugly. We must learn to praise the Lord our God at all times. We must learn to praise Him in the morning, in the noon day, and when the sun goes down. We must learn to praise God for all that He has done, all that He is doing, and all that He is going to do. We must learn to give Him glory for being the Alpha and the Omega. He knows our end from the beginning. Let everything that has breath praise the LORD" (Ps. 150:6)! We must magnify His name forever.

If you just take a moment and reflect back over your life, you will quickly find a reason to praise Him. He is such an awesome wonder! He's perfect in all of His ways. How blessed are we to serve a true and living God. What an honor it is to serve a God who cannot fail. When we begin to praise Jehovah God, even the earth must yield her increase. What does that mean? It means that the earth will also give praise. Everything that is on and in the earth gives praise to God. Can you imagine the whole world praying to God together on one accord at the same time? What a marvelous time that will be!

I encourage you today to stop allowing the enemy to defeat you in your thought process. Go ahead and prophesy to yourself that greater is coming. Know that regardless of how painful your wilderness experience may be, if you can just hold on a little while longer, you're coming out. Do not be moved by what you see! Please have confidence in what God shows you in the spirit. No one else has to know about it. Don't let the enemy trick you out of your blessings. Hold on to every promise that God has given you through His most Holy Word. The more you begin to thank God for His goodness, the more content your heart will become. Before you know it, you will have traded in your spirit of heaviness for a garment of praise; you will have traded your mourning for jars of joy oil (Isa. 61:3).

As children of God, we have to begin to trust God even when what is happening around us makes no sense. Know that when everything comes full circle, you will understand. God knows our end from the beginning. We only know bits and pieces of what God allows us to see. At times it may seem as if things are not going the way we feel like they should. Yet, we have to trust God enough to know that everything is working out for our good. Regardless of what you're believing God for, know that you will receive the answer to your prayer. Hold your head up. God is moving supernaturally on your behalf. This is your time to praise Him in advance. Look past your current circumstances and begin to thank almighty God for His omnipotent power.

I remember the words my mother told me one day. It was in one of her weakest moments. She said, "You know what; if I had died a year ago, I would've been in hell." She admitted that she had been harboring bitterness and unforgiveness. Her relationship with God was very weak. She's a very quiet person by nature and never really got into *praising* the Lord. I was totally shocked by her words one Sunday morning after she pressed her way to church. My mom could barely put one foot in front of the other. She'd lost so much weight that my eyes would sting at the very sight of her. But I knew that my God would use her life as a testimony of His miraculous power.

That Sunday I decided that since she didn't have the

strength to praise the Lord, I would do it for her. I remember running all around the church. You would've thought that I was Flo Jo. I didn't care what people thought. I decided that I was going to praise and worship my God until the walls of Jericho fell down. I danced for my mother's healing; I danced for my ministry; I danced for every good thing that was on its way to me. Had I focused on what I could see in the natural, I would've never left my seat. What I didn't know was while I was running, God was answering. My mother leaned over and told my best friend, "I wish I could run like Kellie. I would run all over the church." My best friend replied, "You are running; you're just using Kellie's legs."

As we talked on the prayer line later that night she told all of us that it's a shame that she had to be laid on her back in order to get her priorities straight. She thanked God that He allowed cancer to enter her body. Now that may sound silly to some, but look at it this way: would it have been better to have died in good health and been sent straight to a devil's hell? God allowed my mother to have a Job experience so that she could receive the gift of eternal life. God places us in the "fire" in order to strengthen our relationship with Him. We must remember that trials come to make us strong, not to tear us down. You will come out without one hair on your head being singed. For that reason alone, you owe God the praise.

Allow me to encourage you today. It doesn't matter what your current circumstance may be. It can appear with your natural eyes that all hope is gone. If you can be bold enough to shout "hallelujah!" anyhow, Jehovah God will meet you where you are. One of my favorite scriptures is 1 Peter 5:10. Let's take a look at it:

> But the God of all grace, who hath called us unto his eternal glory by Christ Jesus, after that ye have suffered a while, make you perfect, stablish, strengthen, settle you.

Does the scripture say after you've suffered forever? No it doesn't. It says after you've suffered a while. Please find comfort in knowing that Jehovah God will allow you to go through a tough time only for a little while. It is during these most difficult times that we are being perfected. It is our time of testing. During this time our faith walk is strengthened. We must be convinced that if God said it in His Word, it *will* come to pass. God will give you a crown of beauty (Isaiah 61:3). God will restore everything that was lost (Joel 2:25). This is your time of testing. Don't fail the test and be pointed back in the direction of the wilderness. Praise Him in the fire. Praise Him through the hurt and the pain. Praise Him during your time of affliction. Never lose hope. If someone dear walks out on you, know that a divine replacement is on the way. Give Him the praise! Thank God for every shut door. It confirms that another one must be opening. Praise Him for the victory now in the mighty name of Jesus!

Let us pray:

*Most gracious and heavenly Father, we thank You,
Lord God, for Your goodness. We celebrate life today,
right where we are. Father, we acknowledge that
nothing compares to You. There is nobody greater than
You, O God. You and You alone are worthy of our
praise. Thank You for this time of testing. Thank You
for perfecting that which concerns us. Thank You for
promising to complete that which You have started.
Thank You for allowing us to trade in our spirits of
heaviness for garments of praise. Hallelujah! We have
prayed. Amen.*

CHAPTER 9

Mission Impossible in Forty Days or Less

Impossible is just a big word thrown around by small men who find it easier to live in the world they've been given than to explore the power they have to change it. Impossible is not a fact. It's an opinion. Impossible is not a declaration. It's a dare. Impossible is potential. Impossible is temporary. Impossible is nothing.

—MUHAMMAD ALI[1]

B EING IN A waiting place is challenging. It may seem as if your entire life has been placed on pause. You may find yourself confused and discouraged. You may feel as if the agony will never end. You sometimes question your petition. You may ask if God will ever work this thing out for you. Will He really do the very thing that you believe Him to do? God is developing you into something greater, and it's going to take a backbreaking experience to pull the best out of you.

Have you ever trained in a gym? When done correctly it is a very challenging experience. When you look around a fitness center you will see all sizes and kinds of people.

Some will focus more on cardio; others will focus more on weights. Some will have mixed routines. The routines vary because it takes different types of training to yield good results for different people. In like manner, your type and extent of training with God will be different from someone else's.

I am heavily into fitness and healthy eating and have been this way most of my life. As I began to get more and more involved in fitness, God gave me a passion to begin to help others achieve optimal health. I then realized that in order to share my expertise with others, I would have to take it up a notch. I decided to hire a personal trainer. On day one I realized that I was nowhere close to where I needed to be. As my personal trainer led me through different routines, he observed my strengths and weakness. He then knew how to customize my fitness plan. Well, if that's what my trainer did in order to help me reach my goals, how do you think our Father in heaven operates? He knows our strengths and weaknesses. As a result, our spiritual fitness plan is customized. I remember times when I felt like I couldn't do another set of reps. My flesh would say, "Give up! Quit!!" but my trainer would be right there coaching me on saying, "Come on, Kellie. You've got to stretch yourself; push!!!" I would try once more, and then he would reach over and help me complete the rep. Just as my trainer helped me complete my tasks after he saw my determination, God will do even more. Our spiritual fitness testing is never to harm us; it's to strengthen us. This reminds me of the scripture in the Book of Matthew:

> And a man with a shriveled hand was there.
> Looking for a reason to accuse Jesus, they asked
> him, "Is it lawful to heal on the Sabbath?" He said
> to them, "If any of you has a sheep and it falls into a
> pit on the Sabbath, will you not take hold of it and
> lift it out. How much more valuable is a man than
> a sheep! Therefore it is lawful to do good on the
> Sabbath. Then he said to the man, "Stretch out your
> hand." So he stretched it out and it was completely
> restored, just as sound as the other.
> —MATTHEW 12:10–13, NIV

Just as the man here in the Book of Matthew stretched
out his withered hand in order to be made whole, God
requires us to stretch. It's not always easy to stretch, espe-
cially when you're already wounded from being in the heat
of battle. Yet, it's an act of faith. Remember, faith is what
moves God.

Now back to the gym. Ever get on the treadmill and
feel as if you're doing a pretty good job? Your headphones
are on; you're bobbing your head to your favorite tunes;
you're actually feeling pretty good. Then, all of a sudden,
someone steps up on the treadmill beside you. The indi-
vidual is nicely toned and looking good. They instantly
start sprinting. Every muscle in their body is flexed. You
wonder how in the world they can run like that. Well,
the truth of the matter is that the person who has the
body you desire did not just wake up one morning that
way. They trained. They prepared. Early in the morning
while others are still sleeping, they are up doing fitness

challenges. While others are chowing down at buffets, they are counting calories and taking in appropriate amounts of protein and other needed nutrients. A physically fit person is a disciplined person. They don't cry and give up at the sight of a challenge. They press on because they have a goal in mind. They know that they are champions and understand the requirements of being a champion.

Believers should apply the same principle. We have to make a decision to live that type of lifestyle. In the face of opposition, we have to keep our focus. Most people recognize a champion only when the world becomes his podium. However, that is not when he actually becomes the champion. He actually became the champion far before. Remember the movie *Rocky*? When did Rocky realize he was a champion? It was actually long before he received the title. Remember how he would run the inclines of the stadium, reach the top, and lift both hands? He didn't wait until he became undefeated; he began to dance his victory dance without an audience. He knew that greatness could not be held down and soon the world would know who he really was.

We too must realize that in order to become a champion we must first gain victory in our daily lives. We must learn to do a "victory dance" while no one is watching. We cannot walk around defeated while waiting on God. We have to know with our knower that we are victors. While others may be living whatever way they want, we must live a life of consecration. Most people only see the champion in his moment of glory. However, it is his lifestyle that actually brought him center stage.

A champion realizes the cost to become great and willingly pays it. You cannot hope to receive great things from God if you don't want to pay the price. We have to decide how badly we want what we want from God. Will we give up and quit when the resistance increases, or will we press on toward the high calling of Jesus Christ? Will we run the stadium as Rocky did and lift our hands toward heaven even before the physical manifestation of our blessings comes? Will we get out there and train no matter the conditions? Will we pray even when we're sleepy? Will we witness to others through our pain? Will we bless others with what little bit we have? The answer must be, "Yes!" All God wants is a *yes!*

We must set goals. When I first met my personal trainer, I didn't allow him to set goals for me. I told him exactly what I wanted and the time frame of which I expected to attain results. Based on what I told him, he put me on a plan called "Mission Impossible in Forty Days or Less." Doesn't that sound painful? Well trust me, it is. However, I wanted what I wanted and I was willing to pay the price to get immediate results. Are you willing to pay the price to get immediate results from God? Are you willing to step out of your comfort zone in order to step into greatness? If you want something bad enough, you will search out what it takes to get it. Fortunately for us, God shows us how to get what we want through His Word and spending time with Him.

However, it will not come without a price. What sacrifices are you willing to make to get God's attention? How much time are you willing to spend in your prayer closet? Do you even have a prayer closet? If not, it's time to find one. Are you willing to sever all ties and inappropriate dealings? Set goals for your life. Decide where you want to be. Write the vision down and make it plain (Hab. 2:2). Ask God to reveal to you a strategic plan of how to gain victory in every area of your life. Ask God to show you what you are to learn during His silence. You may very well be on a "Mission Impossible in Forty Days or Less." Stop crying about it and train! You can do it! You will come out better than ever. Your life will become a wonder to all of those around you. They will know that it was the hand of God upon your life. This is no time to quit. Quitters never win and winners never quit. Embrace the moment; stop complaining.

God is going to do it for you but what are you going to do for God? Once He blesses you, will you go on about your business and forget all that He has done? Don't be like the nine lepers who received their healing and never turned back to say thanks (Luke 17:17). Be the one who will always say, "Thank you, Father, for all the miraculous things that you have done for me."

Remember He knows our end from the beginning. Ask God to remove anything from your heart that will cause you to receive your blessing and then turn away. This is why targeted prayer is so important. We must ask God how to pray effectively and allow the Holy Spirit to make intercession for us. Stretch forth your hand. You are an overcomer! Don't become so overly consumed with your own problems that you miss what God is doing. Being consumed with your problems means that you've taken God out of the driver's seat. Allow God to be God. He's in control. You didn't lay the foundations of the earth! God did. That same God will do what you are believing Him to do if you stop wandering around in the wilderness murmuring and complaining. Be willing to train hard and long. Be willing to make sacrifices while others are sleeping. What you do in secret, God will reward you openly (Matt. 6:6). Allow God to perfect your character. Become a spiritually fit saint—God's champion. Before you know it your deliverance will have come. Praise Jehovah God!

Let us pray:

> *Father God, in the name of Jesus we are making a decision today to stop the murmuring and complaining and to begin our spiritual fitness testing. Give us the ability, O God, to be tenacious. Lord, we understand that this will not be an easy task, but we do know with assurance that You will be right there to coach and encourage us. Thank You in advance for training us up as champions. In You we have victory. In Jesus' name we have prayed. Amen.*

CHAPTER 10

The Strip Down

If you're in anything and never wanted
to quit it, you're not in much.

—T. D. JAKES[1]

A S YOUR BREAKTHROUGH approaches, expect an increase in the intensity of your spiritual testing. It may seem as if the more you pray the more hell breaks loose in your life. If you're not getting a reaction from hell, you should be worried by now. If you are feeling resistance on every side, this is an excellent indicator that your miracle is in close proximity. If you're on track, by now you are probably telling yourself that you'd rather give up than continue in what seems like pure torment.

We must be mindful that although this time of testing is very painful to our flesh, our spirit man is being strengthened. For this reason, we have to remain patient. This is not the time to move out of position because of discomfort. This is actually the time to push through the pain. You must pray through the tears. You must stand on the promises of God no matter how difficult it may be. Know that there is an appointed time for your suffering to end. This set time could very well greet you at daybreak.

While training with my personal trainer one evening, God gave me a divine revelation. I can remember so vividly how I felt that day. It was a cold rainy Sunday; and honestly, I could've stayed in bed. I'd gone to church only to hear a sermon about the importance of marriage and family. Now, of course, most would agree that marriage and family is important. The family is the nucleus of society. If things are out of order at home, you can expect chaos everywhere else. However, when you're beaten down, wounded, and believing God for a complete family, then hearing about the importance of marriage and a complete home hurts. Each time the pastor emphasized the importance of it, my eyes began to burn as I attempted to hold back tears. I was wondering to myself, "How could God allow me to sit and witness this in the midst of my pain?"

What I failed to realize was that God was preparing me for my blessing. I asked myself, "How could the very thing that I'd been praying, fasting, and believing God for be rubbed in my face?" To make matters worse, at the end of the service the pastor called out a young couple who were to marry soon. The entire church prayed for them. I stretched forth my hand through the piercing pain in my heart and honestly thanked God for blessing them with the gift of marriage. I remember crying all the way home. There I was yearning for the very thing that the couple who'd just kneeled down in front of the church was rejoicing about. One thing I had to realize is that all I could see was their victory. I wasn't there to witness the path that the two had to take to reach that point. God never said that the journey would be easy. He never told us that we wouldn't hurt or cry. However, we have the assurance that if God is doing it for others, He will certainly do it for us. just as He promises in the Book of Jeremiah:

> For I know the plans that I think toward you, saith the LORD, thoughts of peace, and not of evil, to give you an expected end.
>
> —JEREMIAH 29:11

After getting home, I cried even harder. I remember burying my head under my pillow. I asked God why I was being tormented. I told God that if He wasn't going to answer me, to just take the desire from me. I was then reminded of the story of Elisha and the Shunammite woman in the Book of 2 Kings. Let's look at it:

> Now it happened one day that Elisha went to Shunem, where there was a notable woman, and she persuaded him to eat some food. So it was, as often as he passed by, he would turn in there to eat some food. And she said to her husband, "Look now, I know that this is a holy man of God, who passes by us regularly. Please, let us make a small upper room on the wall; and let us put a bed for him there, and a table and a chair and a lampstand; so it will be, whenever he comes to us, he can turn in there." And it happened one day that he came there, and he turned in to the upper room and lay down

there. Then he said to Gehazi his servant, "Call this Shunammite woman." When he had called her, she stood before him. And he said to him, "Say now to her, 'Look, you have been concerned for us with all this care. What can I do for you? Do you want me to speak on your behalf to the king or to the commander of the army?'" She answered, "I dwell among my own people." So he said, "What then is to be done for her?" And Gehazi answered, "Actually, she has no son, and her husband is old." So he said, "Call her." When he had called her, she stood in the doorway. Then he said, "About this time next year you shall embrace a son." And she said, "No, my lord. Man of God, do not lie to your maidservant!" But the woman conceived, and bore a son when the appointed time had come, of which Elisha had told her.

—2 KINGS 4: 8–17, NKJV

From reading this text I get the impression that this woman had believed God for a child for so long that she'd rather not talk about it. Have you ever wanted something so badly that you eventually suppressed the desire in order to protect your heart? The Shunammite woman had done this. She immediately told Elisha at his mention of her bringing forth seed not to lie to her. She didn't want to get her hopes up only to be disappointed. Can you relate? Have you ever told God to either do whatever you are believing Him to do or take the desire away? The good news is that God promises in His Word that if we would just delight ourselves in Him, He will grant us the very desires of our heart (Ps. 37:4). Whatever you are believing God to do for you, you must trust that He is a rewarder of those who seek Him whole heartedly (Heb. 11:6). Know and understand that there is an appointed time for you to receive your blessing just as there was an appointed time for the Shunammite woman.

That same evening I met my personal trainer at the gym. My eyes were still puffy from all of the crying I'd done earlier. As if being an emotional wreck was not enough, my trainer decided to increase the difficulty level of my fitness training. After jogging up and down inclines and weight lifting for close to an hour, I was certain that we were about to wrap things up. To my surprise, he then uttered the most dreaded words, "It's time for the strip down." I asked myself, "Now, why would he wait and save the hardest part for last?" Wouldn't it make more sense to do the hardest part first and then ease up as you go? I tried to quickly mentally prepare; but honestly, there's nothing that you can do other than brace yourself for the pain.

You may be wondering, "What is the strip down?" The strip down is the layman's term for "neurological overload sets." During this time you are to painfully push past your muscle fatigue in order to tap into your neurological system. By doing so, you obtain maximum results from your weight training. During the strip down you perform sets of repetitions using weights with about a 15–20 percent reduction in strength training every forty seconds or so. For instance, if you start weight lifting at sixty pounds, you will do about twelve reps or so, pause for about forty seconds, and then go to forty pounds and do twelve reps or so, then twenty pounds, etc., until you get to zero. You take a break and then you start the second phase. During the second phase there are no breaks and no set amount of reps. The trainer then observes you; and when he sees that you can no longer keep your form due to pain, he lightens the load and then you're on to the next set. During this time, the lactic acid from your muscles will begin to burn. Everything in you will say, "Quit"; but because you've tapped into your neurological system, you're able to override the way your body actually feels and continue on. By the time you get to the last set at zero pounds, it feels as if you're lifting seventy-five pounds. So how do you finish the set? You somehow reach deep within yourself and continue in spite of the pain because you know that the end is near. By this time, you're almost done; you've come too far to give up now. So you brace yourself and give it all you've got. Next thing you know, you're done with the strip down.[2]

You may be wondering what the correlation is between the strip down and your breakthrough. When you're believing God for a miracle, don't lose out at the expense of your flesh. You must tap into the strength of your spirit man. Your flesh will feel the pain of waiting but the Spirit of God that resides on the inside of you is so much greater. If a personal trainer cares enough about his client to lighten the load once the struggle becomes too great, what more would our Father in heaven do for us? When He sees that we cannot endure any more pain, He performs a spiritual weight reduction. Not only does He lighten the load, but—unlike my trainer—God also renews our strength. Brace yourself; give the Lord all that you have; complete the "spiritual strip down." Before you know it, the session is over, the pain is gone, and your miracle has been received.

Let's pray:

> *Father God, in the name of Jesus, we thank You for our time of spiritual testing. We also thank You, Lord God, for the gift of the Holy Spirit. For it is Your Spirit that empowers us to be tenacious. We thank You, Lord, that as we complete our "spiritual strip down" our miracle awaits us at daybreak. We confirm that nothing, no matter how difficult the task, will separate us from Your love. In Jesus' name we have prayed. Amen.*

CHAPTER 11

Open the Door

*For a great door and effectual is opened unto
me, and there are many adversaries.*

—1 CORINTHIANS 16:9

COULD THE ANSWER to your prayer be knocking at your door? Do you realize that things happen when the church prays without ceasing? You must be persistent. If persistence was not required, the story of the persistent widow would have to be removed from the Bible. It doesn't matter if the answer has been *no* a thousand times. It doesn't matter if all those who initially started out cheering you on have now left the stands. Keep the faith. You *will* win. You will soon open the door to your answered prayer. I know it may be difficult for you to believe right now, but God has heard you. This is the exact scenario that takes place in the Book of Acts.

The church was fervently praying for Peter to be released from prison. While they were yet praying, the answer to their prayer knocked on the door. I decree and declare the same for you. While you are yet praying, doors are swinging wide open. Let's take a look at what happened when the church prayed in the Book of Acts:

> Now about that time Herod the king stretched forth his hands to vex certain of the church. And he killed James the brother of John with the sword. And because he saw it pleased the Jews, he proceeded further to take Peter also. (Then were the days of unleavened bread.) And when he had apprehended him, he put him in prison, and delivered him to four quaternions of soldiers to keep him; intending after Easter to bring him forth to the people. Peter therefore was kept in prison: **but prayer was made without ceasing of the church unto God for him**. And when Herod would have brought him forth, the same night Peter was sleeping between two soldiers, bound with two chains: and the keepers before the door kept the prison. And, behold, the angel of the Lord came upon him, and a light shined in the prison: and he smote Peter on the side, and raised him up, saying, Arise up quickly. And his chains fell off from his hands. And the angel said unto him, Gird thyself, and bind on thy sandals. And so he did. And he saith unto him, Cast thy garment about thee, and follow me. And he went out, and followed him; and wist not that it was true which was done by the angel; but thought he saw a vision. When they were past the first and the second ward, they came unto the iron gate that leadeth unto the city; which opened to them of his own accord: and they went out, and passed on through one street; and forthwith the angel departed from him. And when

Peter was come to himself, he said; now I know of a surety, that the Lord hath sent his angel, and hath delivered me out of the hand of Herod, and from all the expectation of the people of the Jews. And when he had considered the thing, he came to the house of Mary the mother of John, whose surname was Mark; where many were gathered together praying. And as Peter knocked at the door of the gate, a damsel came to hearken, named Rhoda. And when she knew Peter's voice, she opened not the gate for gladness, but ran in, and told how Peter stood before the gate. And they said unto her, Thou art mad. But she constantly affirmed that it was even so. Then said they, It is his angel. **But Peter continued knocking**: and when they had opened the door, and saw him, they were astonished. But he, beckoning unto them with the hand to hold their peace, declared unto them how the Lord had brought him out of the prison. And he said, Go shew these things unto James, and to the brethren. And he departed, and went into another place.

—ACTS 12:1–17, EMPHASIS ADDED

The church was so busy praying for Peter's release that they failed to realize that the very thing that they believed God for came and knocked on the door. When Peter knocked Rhoda came to the door; and instead of opening it, she ran away astonished.

I decree and declare right now in the name of Jesus that when your true blessing arrives, you too will be astonished and all of those around you. Remember, God loves an audience. Sometimes He allows things to get ugly so that all of your spectators will know without a shadow of a doubt that it was His hand upon your life. Remember, when God is for you, who can be against you (Rom. 8:31).

What happened when the damsel ran away instead of opening the door for Peter? Did Peter turn away? No, he did not; he continued knocking until the door was opened. When the church saw Peter they were amazed. Peter quickly asked them to hold their peace as he began to testify of the goodness of the Lord. He immediately proclaimed that it was God who opened the prison doors and released him.

I decree and declare that the same God who heard the cries of the church and released Peter from the chains that had him bound will do the very same thing for you. This is why you must stand in faith. Against all odds, you too will soon have a testimony. The angels assigned to release your blessing will not stop until you've been located. You're too close to hearing a knock on your door to get out of position now. The Book of Judges teaches us that you can be out of place when the blessing comes. Let's take a look:

> And there was a certain man of Zorah, of the family of the Danites, whose name was Manoah; and his wife was barren, and bare not. And the angel of the LORD appeared unto the woman, and said unto her, Behold now, thou art barren, and bearest not: but thou shalt conceive, and bear a son. Now therefore beware, I pray thee, and drink not wine nor strong drink, and eat not any unclean thing: For, lo, thou

shalt conceive, and bear a son; and no razor shall come on his head: for the child shall be a Nazarite unto God from the womb: and he shall begin to deliver Israel out of the hand of the Philistines. Then the woman came and told her husband, saying, a man of God came unto me, and his countenance was like the countenance of an angel of God, very terrible: but I asked him not whence he was, neither told he me his name. But he said unto me, Behold, thou shalt conceive, and bear a son; and now drink no wine nor strong drink, neither eat any unclean thing: for the child shall be a Nazarite to God from the womb to the day of his death. Then Manoah intreated the Lord, and said, O my Lord, let the man of God which thou didst send come again unto us, and teach us what we shall do unto the child that shall be born. And God hearkened to the voice of Manoah; and the angel of God came again unto the woman as she sat in the field: but Manoah her husband was not with her.

—Judges 13:2–9

This scripture confirms that we should expect that which we've prayed for. However, we must not be out of position to receive. With God there is no concept of time, meaning we have no way of knowing when God will answer. Yet we can be assured that God will answer in due season. Just as God hearkened unto the voice of Manoah, He will also hearken unto your voice. Trust that God has heard you and is ready to send the blessing to your doorstep. It doesn't matter what it looks like. It doesn't matter if the enemy of your soul is attempting to make a mockery out of you. Build your ark in faith; the rain will eventually fall. Remember, weeping may endure for a night, but joy comes in the morning (Ps. 30:5). The same Jesus that turned water into wine is transforming your tears into full-scale laughter right now. The fact that you can't see it with your natural eyes means absolutely nothing. The enemy may be asking you, "Where is your God?" Rebuke him in Jesus' name. Your God will surely step in on time. When Jesus was at the wedding feast and they ran out of wine, what happened? Let's look at it:

> And the third day there was a marriage in Cana of Galilee; and the mother of Jesus was there: And both Jesus was called, and his disciples, to the marriage. And when they wanted wine, the mother of Jesus saith unto him, they have no wine. Jesus saith unto her, Woman, what have I to do with thee? Mine hour is not yet come. His mother saith unto the servants, whatsoever he saith unto you, do it. And there were set there six waterpots of stone, after the manner of the purifying of the Jews, containing two or three firkins apiece. Jesus saith unto them, Fill the waterpots with water. And they filled them up to the brim.
>
> —John 2:1–7

You may be wondering why Jesus was even at a wedding feast in the first place. In those days many times the whole town would attend weddings. It was considered an insult to refuse an invitation. As a result, an event such as this required careful planning. The host was to provide enough wine to last for seven days. To run out of wine at a wedding would have been a social blunder that would have been a source of embarrassment to the family for years. What does that tell you about our God? When the enemy is attempting to make a social blunder out of you, trust and believe that God will never allow you to be put to shame. When Mary told Jesus there was no wine, Jesus then asked His mother what He had to do with this since His hour had not yet come. What he meant was His plan was not to begin doing miracles until He began his journey to the cross. Please note that Jesus never said yes. Yet Mary tuned to the servants and told them, "Do whatever He tells you." She then walked away.

If you know that you've been obedient, you too may have to walk away sometimes in order to receive your miracle. You may come to a point where you've done all you can and yet the door to your answered prayer has been slammed shut. This is when you are to throw your hands up and surrender. Tell God, "This is it!" You're staying in position and trusting Him to do just what He promised.

It was not until after Mary walked away that Jesus gave the instructions to the servants to fill the jars with water. Each jar holding twenty or thirty gallons were then filled to the brim. Now imagine that for a moment. In those days there was no running water. So the servants obviously had to go back and forth from a water source over and over until each jar was filled. I'm sure they came to a point of weariness. They made trip after trip, yet the water remained water.

The water did not turn to wine until after all six stone water jars had been filled and were ready to be drawn out for the governor to taste. Did that not require faith? Yes it did. The servants were obedient to the instructions of Jesus and experienced a transformation. There is no way of knowing where in the process of going back and forth with water that the miracle took place. Was it during the trips, or was it as they began to pour the water? That we do not know. But what we do know is that a miracle did take place. The same goes for us. We don't know when the transformation will take place. We don't know the appointed time for our water to turn to wine. Yet, we must have the faith to know that it will.

Let us pray:

> *Father God, we understand the power of a church that prays. We humbly ask for the gates of our spiritual ears to be opened so that we may hear the knock at the door and openly receive the answers to our prayers. We know that regardless of what it looks like, blessing angels have been released from heaven and are in route to our doorsteps. We know that a miracle is taking place and soon our water will turn to wine. Allow us to trust and depend totally on You. If we've been doing things in our own strength, forgive us. In Jesus' name we have prayed. Amen.*

CHAPTER 12

Alternate Ending

*I believe that God's gifts and blessings are
abundantly laid before us. Most of the time, it's
up to us to find our way to them. God has done
His part and it's up to us to complete the task.*

—ARINA NIKITINA[1]

Declaring the end from the beginning, and from
ancient times the things that are not yet done,
saying, my counsel shall stand, and I will do all my
pleasure.

—ISAIAH 46:10

Have you ever walked away from a movie wishing
for an alternate ending? You watched in anticipation
with popcorn in hand. Then all of a sudden the script takes
an unexpected turn. You find yourself thinking, "This can't
be the end! They could've done better than that!" Perhaps the movie you watched was a sequel to your favorite
movie. Your expectations were set high. You rushed out
and bought tickets early. You waited in line out in the cold
for hours without one murmur or complaint. Yet you left

79

the theater unfulfilled. Thank God that this only happens in movies, right? Well, maybe.

Ponder this question for a moment. What happens when the script of your life takes an unexpected turn? You know, when life throws you a curve ball? Perhaps you had it all planned out. You would marry the perfect person, raise the perfect family, live in the perfect home, enjoy perfect health, and enjoy the best job on earth. But then something happened. You didn't see it coming. Everything was going just fine, and then all of a sudden without warning the bottom fell out. All of your hopes and dreams traveled south and you found your life in a mess.

Perhaps that once so perfect marriage turned into hell on earth right before your eyes and you were faced with the embarrassment of divorce. What happens when the once so perfect job is now stressing you out beyond belief? What do you do when your perfect child becomes not so perfect? What happens when even those in your inner circle are secretly planning your demise? Do you fold? Think about it. What happens when you'd rather censor your personal testimony than let others know about all of the hell that you are actually going through? What do you do when you're doing everything you can to hold things together and without sympathy the world keeps pounding on you. Your heart is aching with disappointment; so many "what ifs." Had I only done this or done that. You feel defeated. Yet those who want to see you fail are viscously leaning over you trying to check a pulse. Do you accept it or do you rise up out of your ashes so that God will get the glory out of your story?

Well, let me encourage you to rise up! You must know who lives on the inside of you. You must know that the joy of the Lord is your strength (Neh. 8:10). He is your strong Tower. This is a time to rejoice! You no longer have to hide and run from your past. Trade in your sorrow for His joy. He is with you. No matter how bad it gets, God is with you. When you're in the fire, He's right there with you. When the storms are raging in your life, He is right there with you. When the whole world has turned its back on you, God is with you. In and out of season, Jehovah God is with you. When the doctors give you a bad report, know that God is with you. When you least expect it, God will show up mightily in your life. Your joy will soon become full. I decree and declare it in the name of Jesus. You will laugh again! God says in His Word, "I have been young, and now am old; yet have I not seen the righteous forsaken, nor his seed begging bread" (Ps. 37:25). You must have the assurance the Jehovah God has your back.

You are not forgotten. God knows you by name. He will do what's best for you. We must understand that it would be poor parenting if God released everything to us in a way that we feel like He should. What if what you've been praying for could later harm you? What if what you're believing God for does not line up with His perfect will for your life? You do want His perfect will right? We have to be willing to accept an alternate ending—the better ending. Maybe your life has not unfolded as you felt like it should. Yet you must take solace in the fact that God is working it out. You have to believe it. Remember, the Bible teaches us that all things work together for our good. So that means the good, the bad, and the ugly. Unlike your favorite movie, God will not leave you disappointed or unfilled. God is a restorer. Receive that restoration now in Jesus name. For it is written:

> Thou, which hast shewed me great and sore troubles, shalt quicken me again, and shalt bring me up again from the depths of the earth. Thou shalt increase my greatness, and comfort me on every side. I will also praise thee with the psaltery, even thy truth, O my God: unto thee will I sing with the harp, O thou Holy One of Israel. My lips shall greatly rejoice when I sing unto thee; and my soul, which thou hast redeemed. My tongue also shall talk of thy righteousness all the day long: for they are confounded, for they are brought unto shame that seek my hurt.
>
> —PSALM 71:20–24

You must know that whatever you've been crying out to God about has been heard. If you have been heard, you too will be answered! Search your heart. Could the answer be right in front of you?

Cross references:

A. Psalm 71:1: 71:1–3; 31:1–4
B. Psalm 71:1: Deut. 23:15; Ruth 2:12
C. Psalm 71:1: 22:5

D. Psalm 71:2: 2 Kings 19:16
E. Psalm 71:3: 18:2
F. Psalm 71:4: 2 Kings 19:19
G. Psalm 71:4: 140:4
H. Psalm 71:4: Gen. 48:16
I. Psalm 71:5: 9:18; 25:5
J. Psalm 71:5: Job 4:6; Jer. 17:7
K. Psalm 71:6: 22:10
L. Psalm 71:6: 22:9; Job 3:16
M. Psalm 71:6: 9:1; 34:1; 52:9; 119:164; 145:2
N. Psalm 71:7: Deut. 28:46; Isa. 8:18; 1 Cor. 4:9
O. Psalm 71:7: 61:3; 2 Sam. 22:3
P. Psalm 71:8: 71:15; 51:15; 63:5
Q. Psalm 71:8: 96:6; 104:1
R. Psalm 71:9: 51:11
S. Psalm 71:9: 92:14; Isa. 46:4
T. Psalm 71:9: Deut. 4:31; 31:6
U. Psalm 71:10: 3:7
V. Psalm 71:10: 10:8; 59:3; Prov. 1:18
W. Psalm 71:10: 31:13; Exod. 1:10; Matt. 12:14
X. Psalm 71:11: 9:10; 54:7; Isa. 40:27; Lam. 5:20; Matt. 27:46
Y. Psalm 71:11: 7:2
Z. Psalm 71:12: 38:21
AA. Psalm 71:12: 22:19; 38:22
AB. Psalm 71:13: Jer. 18:19
AC. Psalm 71:13: 25:3; Job 8:22
AD. Psalm 71:13: 70:2
AE. Psalm 71:14: 25:3; 42:5; 130:7; 131:3
AF. Psalm 71:15: 71:8; 66:16
AG. Psalm 71:15: 51:14
AH. Psalm 71:16: 9:1; 77:12; 106:2; 118:15; 145:4

AI. Psalm 71:17: Deut. 4:5; Jer. 7:13
AJ. Psalm 71:17: 26:7; 86:10; 96:3; Job 5:9
AK. Psalm 71:18: Isa. 46:4
AL. Psalm 71:18: Exod. 9:16
AM. Psalm 71:18: 22:30–31; 78:4; 145:4; Job 8:8; Joel 1:3
AN. Psalm 71:19: 36:5
AO. Psalm 71:19: 126:2; Luke 1:49
AP. Psalm 71:19: 35:10; 77:13; 89:8
AQ. Psalm 71:20: 25:17
AR. Psalm 71:20: 80:3, 19; 85:4; Hosea 6:2
AS. Psalm 71:20: 63:9
AT. Psalm 71:21: 18:35
AU. Psalm 71:21: 23:4; 86:17; Isa. 12:1; 40:1–2; 49:13; 54:10
AV. Psalm 71:22: 33:2
AW. Psalm 71:22: 144:9; 92:3; Job 21:12
AX. Psalm 71:22: 2 Kings 19:22
AY. Psalm 71:23: 20:5
AZ. Psalm 71:23: Exod. 15:13
BA. Psalm 71:24: 35:28
BB. Psalm 71:24: 71:13
BC. Psalm 71:24: Esther 9:2[2]

Could it be that you've been asking God for a purple ball but He's already placed a red ball right in your front yard? Can you become so fixed on the color of the ball that you fail to recognize that the answer has been released? After all, you were asking for a ball right? Is He not trying to give you a ball? Maybe God chose to give you the red ball because the purple ball would later roll into the street and cause you to get run over as you chased it. Think about it for a minute. What if what you're asking for may later run you over? God loves us so much that He knows what's best. Let's look at what Scripture says to support this:

> If a son shall ask bread of any of you that is a father, will he give him a stone? or if he asks a fish, will he for a fish give him a serpent? Or if he shall ask an egg, will he offer him a scorpion? If ye then, being evil, know how to give good gifts unto your children: how much more shall your heavenly Father give the Holy Spirit to them that ask him?
>
> —LUKE 11:11–13

I've prayed this prayer point many a nights but it wasn't until one of my best friends came to minister to me early one morning that I received the revelation. You see, I too was believing God for the purple ball. I was so convinced that it was what I wanted and needed. I wouldn't even entertain the thought of any other color ball. It wasn't until the purple ball decided to roll into the street that I had to make a decision. Do I continue after the ball knowing that it could cost my joy, my peace, my happiness, my ministry, and my life; or do I walk away from it?

After my friend sat me down and said, "Kellie, how do you know that what you're asking for is not stone and God has been trying to give you bread?" That's when I realized that she could be right. All along I was so caught up in my own strategic plan that I didn't realize that I was trying to work everything out in my own strength. I failed to recognize the jewel that was standing right in front of me because I was so fixed on what I thought I wanted. I was believing God but still trying to help Him out. You know how we sometimes do. We ask God to perform a miracle but when it doesn't happen fast enough, we move ahead of Him in an effort to speed up the process. What am I saying? God loves us so much that He will not release something to us that will later harm us. That also includes releasing a blessing too soon. We only know in part. It is God who knows our end from our beginning. Father knows best.

Take a moment and ask yourself, "Am I moving ahead of God? Am I too fixated on what I think should happen that I'm refusing to accept the possibility of an alternate ending?" Remember, God is sovereign. He can do what He wants when He wants. When it looks as if nothing is happening, know that God is moving behind the scenes. Do not allow the enemy of your soul to come in and throw you off course. Allow God's perfect will to be done in your life. His answer to your prayer will be far better than anything you could've ever imagined. Trust God. He will bring it to pass. Ask yourself, "Is God still silent or am I ignoring the signs?" Your answer could be staring you right in the face. Surrender your will to His today and allow God to bless you. Receive the answer to your prayer. Do not allow its color, texture, or packaging to cause you to miss out. Be encouraged. Receive God's best. For it is written:

Eye hath not seen, nor ear heard, neither have entered into the heart of man, the things which God hath prepared for them that love him.

—1 Corinthians 2:9

Let us pray:

Father God, we thank You and accept Your perfect will for our lives. We are now ready to receive Your best even if Your best results in an alternate ending. If we are asking for stone, give us the heart to change our prayer so that we may receive bread. Do not allow us to miss the answers to our prayers because of their packaging. We are no longer ashamed of our past mistakes. We understand that You allowed us to go through those difficult times in order to bring You glory. Lord, we love You and are excited about the future that we have in You. We know that there is an expected end, and we thank You sincerely for it. Father, we lean not to our own understanding. We stand ready to receive the life that only You can provide for us. In Jesus' name. Amen.

Scriptures for Answered Prayer

- John 15:7: "If ye abide in me, and my words abide in you, ye shall ask what ye will, and it shall be done unto you."

- Psalm 66:18: "If I regard iniquity in my heart, the Lord will not hear me."

- James 4:3: "Ye ask, and receive not, because ye ask amiss, that ye may consume it upon your lusts."

- 1 John 5:14–15: "And this is the confidence that we have in him that, if we ask any thing according to his will he heareth us."

- Mark 11:24: "Therefore I say unto you, What things soever ye desire, when ye pray, believe that ye receive them, and ye shall have them."

- Hebrews 11:6: "But without faith it is impossible to please him: for he that cometh to God must believe that he is, and that he is a rewarder of them that diligently seek him."

- 1 John 3:22: "And whatsoever we ask, we receive of him, because we keep his commandments, and do those things that are pleasing in his sight."

- Hebrews 11:1: "Now faith is the substance of things hoped for, the evidence of things not seen."

- James 1:6–7: "But let him ask in faith, nothing wavering. For he that wavereth is like a wave of the sea driven with the wind and tossed. For let not that man think that he shall receive any thing of the Lord."

- James 4:2: "Ye lust, and have not: ye kill, and desire to have, and cannot obtain: ye fight and war, yet ye have not, because ye ask not."

- Matthew 7:7: "Ask, and it shall be given you; seek, and ye shall find; knock, and it shall be opened unto you."

- James 5:16: "Confess your faults one to another, and pray one for another, that ye may be healed. The effectual fervent prayer of a righteous man availeth much."

- 1 Thessalonians 5:17: "Pray without ceasing."

- Ephesians 6:18: "Praying always with all prayer and supplication in the Spirit, and watching thereunto with all perseverance and supplication for all saints."

- Romans 15:13: "Now the God of hope fill you with all joy and peace in believing, that ye may abound in hope, through the power of the Holy Ghost."

- John 16:24: "Hitherto have ye asked nothing in my name: ask, and ye shall receive, that your joy may be full."

- John 3:16: "For God so loved the world, that he gave his only begotten Son, that whosoever believeth in him should not perish, but have everlasting life."

- 1 John 1:9: "If we confess our sins, he is faithful and just to forgive us our sins, and to cleanse us from all unrighteousness."

- James 1:6: "But let him ask in faith, nothing wavering. For he that wavereth is like a wave of the sea driven with the wind and tossed."

- Philippians 4:6: "Be careful for nothing; but in every thing by prayer and supplication with thanksgiving let your requests be made known unto God."

- Ephesians 6:12: "For we wrestle not against flesh and blood, but against principalities, against powers, against the rulers of the darkness of this world, against spiritual wickedness in high places."

- Ephesians 2:8–9: "For by grace are ye saved through faith; and that not of yourselves: it is the gift of God. Not of works, lest any man should boast."

- Galatians 6:9: "And let us not be weary in well doing: for in due season we shall reap, if we faint not."

- John 15:16: "Ye have not chosen me, but I have chosen you, and ordained you, that ye should go and bring forth fruit, and that your fruit should remain: that whatsoever ye shall ask of the Father in my name, he may give it you."

- John 14:13–14: "And whatsoever ye shall ask in my name, that will I do, that the Father may be glorified in the Son. If ye shall ask any thing in my name, I will do it."

- Luke 11:9: "And I say unto you, Ask, and it shall be given you; seek, and ye shall find; knock, and it shall be opened unto you."

- Mark 11:23: "For verily I say unto you, That whosoever shall say unto this mountain, Be thou removed, and be thou cast into the sea; and shall not doubt in his heart, but shall believe that those things which he saith shall come to pass; he shall have whatsoever he saith."

- Matthew 21:21: "Jesus answered and said unto them, Verily I say unto you, If ye have faith, and doubt not, ye shall not only do this which is done to the fig tree, but also if ye shall say unto this mountain, Be thou removed, and be thou cast into the sea; it shall be done."

- Matthew 6:6: "But thou, when thou prayest, enter into thy closet, and when thou hast shut thy door, pray to thy Father which is in secret; and thy Father which seeth in secret shall reward thee openly."

- Jude 1:20: "But ye, beloved, building up yourselves on your most holy faith, praying in the Holy Ghost."

- 1 John 5:14: "And this is the confidence that we have in him, that, if we ask any thing according to his will, he heareth us."

- 1 Peter 3:12: "For the eyes of the Lord are over the righteous, and his ears are open unto their prayers: but the face of the Lord is against them that do evil."

- Romans 10:17: "So then faith cometh by hearing, and hearing by the word of God."

- John 9:31: "Now we know that God heareth not sinners: but if any man be a worshipper of God, and doeth his will, him he heareth."

- Luke 18:1: "And he spake a parable unto them to this end, that men ought always to pray, and not to faint."

- Matthew 21:22: "And all things, whatsoever ye shall ask in prayer, believing, ye shall receive."

- Matthew 7:7–8: "Ask, and it shall be given you; seek, and ye shall find; knock, and it shall be opened unto you. For every one that asketh receiveth; and he that seeketh findeth; and to him that knocketh it shall be opened."

- Proverbs 21:13: "Whoso stoppeth his ears at the cry of the poor, he also shall cry himself, but shall not be heard."

- Proverbs 15:29: "The LORD is far from the wicked: but he heareth the prayer of the righteous."

- 2 Chronicles 7:14: "If my people, which are called by my name, shall humble themselves, and pray, and seek my face, and turn from their wicked ways; then will I hear from heaven, and will forgive their sin, and will heal their land."

- James 2:20: "But wilt thou know, O vain man, that faith without works is dead?"

- Galatians 5:6: "For in Jesus Christ neither circumcision availeth anything, nor uncircumcision; but faith which worketh by love."

- Romans 10:9–10: "That if thou shalt confess with thy mouth the Lord Jesus, and shalt believe in thine heart that God hath raised him from the dead, thou shalt be saved. For with the heart man believeth unto righteousness; and with the mouth confession is made unto salvation."

- Acts 16:25: "And at midnight Paul and Silas prayed, and sang praises unto God: and the prisoners heard them."

- Acts 14:23: "And when they had ordained them elders in every church, and had prayed with fasting, they commended them to the Lord, on whom they believed."

- John 14:1, 13–14: "Let not your heart be troubled: ye believe in God, believe also in me."

- John 14:13–14: "And whatsoever ye shall ask in my name, that will I do, that the Father may be glorified in the Son. If ye shall ask any thing in my name, I will do it."

- Luke 11:1: "And it came to pass, that, as he was praying in a certain place, when he ceased, one of his disciples said unto him, Lord, teach us to pray, as John also taught his disciples."

- Luke 6:12: "And it came to pass in those days, that he went out into a mountain to pray, and continued all night in prayer to God."

- Mark 12:30–31: "And thou shalt love the Lord thy God with all thy heart, and with all thy soul, and with all thy mind, and with all thy strength: this is the first commandment. And the second is like, namely this, Thou shalt love thy neighbour as thyself. There is none other commandment greater than these."

- Matthew 11:28: "Come unto me, all ye that labour and are heavy laden, and I will give you rest."

- James 4:8–10: "Draw nigh to God, and he will draw nigh to you. Cleanse your hands, ye sinners; and purify your hearts, ye double minded. Be afflicted, and mourn, and weep: let your laughter be turned to mourning, and your joy to heaviness. Humble yourselves in the sight of the Lord, and he shall lift you up."

- 1 Corinthians 7:5: "Defraud ye not one the other, except it be with consent for a time, that ye may give yourselves to fasting and prayer; and come together again, that Satan tempt you not for your incontinency."

- Romans 12:2: "And be not conformed to this world: but be ye transformed by the renewing of your mind, that ye may prove what is that good, and acceptable, and perfect, will of God."

Notes

Introduction

1. C. S. Lewis quote found at Good Reads, http://www.goodreads.com/quotes/28672-i-know-now-lord-why-you-utter-no-answer-you (accessed June 28, 2013).

Chapter 1: Why Is Heaven Shut Up?

1. T. D. Jakes quote found at Inspirational Quote, http://www.inspirational-quote.com/td-jakes-quotes.html (accessed June 29, 2013).

Chapter 2: Faith and a Dime

1. Charles Wesley quote found at Brainy Quote, http://www.brainyquote.com/quotes/quotes/c/charleswes187239.html (accessed June 29, 2013).

Chapter 3: Warning: Watch Your Mouth

1. Joel Osteen quote found at Search Quotes, http://www.searchquotes.com/quotation/You_can_change_your_world_by_changing_your_words..._Remember,_death_and_life_are_in_the_power_of_the/2851/ (accessed June 29, 2013).

Chapter 4: Don't Put God in the Trunk

1. Star1949, "God Can ride in the Trunk! Remember the e-mail?" Red Bubble, http://www.redbubble.com/people/starr1949/writing/301906-god-can-ride-in-the-trunk-remember-the-e-mail (accessed June 29, 2013).

Chapter 5: Pace Yourself

1. Juma Ikangaa quote found at Inspirational Quotes, http://www.trevianxc.com/trevianxc.com/Inspirational_Quotes.html (accessed June 29, 2013).
2. Brad, "How to Train for a Marathon or Half Marathon," Marathon Rookie, http://www.marathonrookie.com/ (accessed June 29, 2013).

Chapter 6: Help!

1. St. Frances De Sales quote found at Search Quotes, http://www
.searchquotes.com/quotation/We_shall_steer_safely_through_
every_storm,_so_long_as_our_heart_is_right,_our_intention_
fervent,_our/1009/ (accessed June 30, 2013).

Chapter 7: A Delayed Blessing

1. T. D. Jakes quote found at Inspirational Quote, http://www
.inspirational-quote.com/td-jakes-quotes.html (accessed June 30,
2013).

Chapter 8: Praise Him in the Fire

1. Don McMinn, quoted in LaMar Boschman, *A Heart of Worship*
(Lake Mary, FL: Creation House, 1994) 60, found at The Choice
Driven Life, http://www.thechoicedrivenlife.com/quotes-on-
choices/worship/ (accessed June 30, 2013).

Chapter 9: Mission Impossible in Forty Days or Less

1. Muhammad Ali quote found at Good Reads, http://www
.goodreads.com/quotes/121663-impossible-is-just-a-big-word-
thrown-around-by-small (accessed June 30, 2013).

Chapter 10: The Strip Down

1. T. D. Jakes quote found at Inspirational Quote, http://www
.inspirational-quote.com/td-jakes-quotes.html (accessed June 30,
2013).
2. Ben Pakulski, "Neurological Overload Set (NOS)," Bodybuilding
Articles: The Science of Building Muscle and Losing Fat, http://
www.bodybuildingarticles.net/2011/11/neurological-overload-set-
nos-ben.html (accessed June 30, 2013).

Chapter 12: Alternate Ending

1. Arina Nikitina, "Delaying God's Blessings," Goal Setting Guide,
http://www.goal-setting-guide.com/delaying-gods-blessings
(accessed July 1, 2013).
2. Scripture reference list found at http://www.biblegateway.com/
passage/?search=Psalm%2071&version=NIV#cen-NIV-14978B
(accessed July 1, 2013).

About the Author

KELLIE LANE IS a passionate communicator and orator of God's Word with a great desire to motivate His people to reach their maximum potential in Jesus Christ. It is her heartfelt desire for all to connect with and experience God's love and plan for their lives. She is a free-lance writer, author, motivational speaker, prayer warrior, and minister of dance. Kellie graduated from the University Of Mississippi Medical Center School Of Nursing with a Bachelor of Science in Nursing (2002) and a Master of Science in Nursing (2006). She is currently working to complete her Doctor of Nursing Practice Degree at the University of Mississippi. She is a wife and has been blessed with six children. She is a spiritual mother to many more.

Contact the Author

www.kellielane.org

47906750R00064

Made in the USA
Middletown, DE
05 September 2017